This and That

by Vic Warren Illustrated by Olivia Cole

$$2 + 2 = 4$$

tooth + brush = toothbrush

SRA

SRA/McGraw–Hill

Columbus, Ohio

I bet you know all about adding numbers. But what do you know about adding words?

2+2 = 4

tooth + brush = toothbrush

Take some **butter.**
Add a **fly.**
Now you have a...

butterfly.

4

Put a **foot**
with a **ball.**
Now you have a...

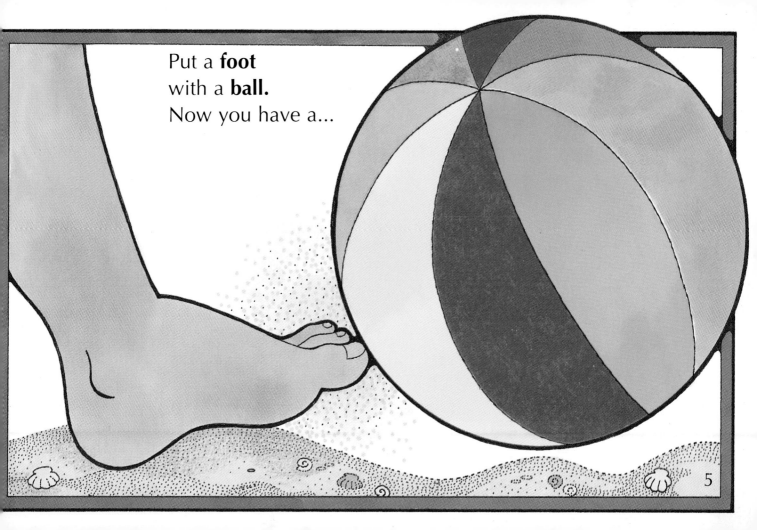

football.

6

Take a **pan**
and a **cake.**
Now you have a...

pancake.

rainbow.

10

Add a **cup**
and a **board.**
Now you have a...

cupboard.

Put a **star**
with a **fish.**
Now you have a...

13

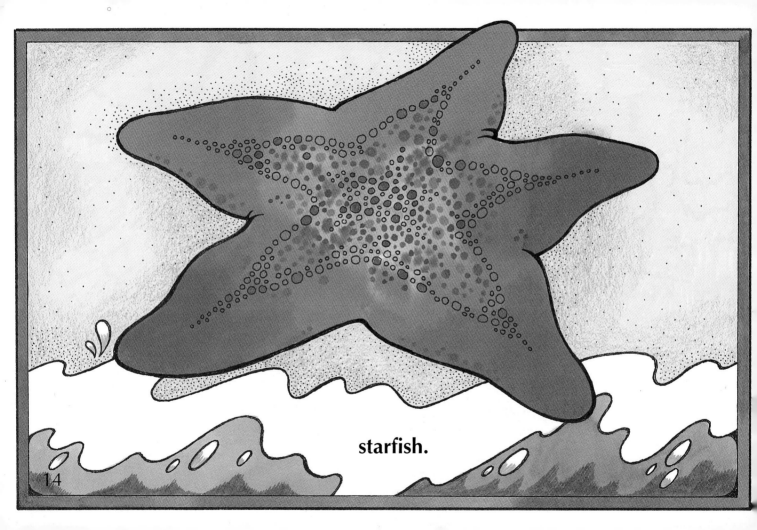

starfish.

Take a **book.**
Find the **end.**
Now you have a...

THE END

DOGS

15

bookend.